SERVANT LEADERSHIP LESSONS FROM THE LIFE OF GENERAL Y. K. MUSEVENI.

SERVANT LEADERSHIP LESSONS FROM THE LIFE OF GENERAL Y. K. MUSEVENI.

TONY AKAKI

SERVANT LEADERSHIP LESSONS FROM THE LIFE OF GENERAL Y. K. MUSEVENI.

iUniverse books may be ordered through booksellers or by contacting:

iUniverse
1663 Liberty Drive
Bloomington, IN 47403
www.iuniverse.com
844-349-9409

Because of the dynamic nature of the Internet, any web addresses or links contained in this book may have changed since publication and may no longer be valid. The views expressed in this work are solely those of the author and do not necessarily reflect the views of the publisher, and the publisher hereby disclaims any responsibility for them.

Any people depicted in stock imagery provided by Getty Images are models, and such images are being used for illustrative purposes only.
Certain stock imagery © Getty Images.

ISBN: 978-1-6632-1801-8 (sc)
ISBN: 978-1-6632-1800-1 (e)

Print information available on the last page.

iUniverse rev. date: 02/05/2021

To

Betty Amongi and all other self-seeking
politicians that work for themselves.

Quotes

I hear some people saying that I'm their servant, I'm not a servant of anybody. I am a freedom fighter, I'm not your servant. I am fighting for myself and for my beliefs. That's how I come in. I'm not an employee. General Yoweri Kaguta Museveni, January 2017

I'm working for myself, I'm not working for other people, I'm working for my grandchildren, for my children." – General Yoweri Kaguta Museveni, July 2018

I pledge to be your servant once I assume presidency. Robert Kyagulanyi aka Bobi Wine, November 2020

Not so with you. Instead, whoever wants to become great among you must be your servant, and whoever wants to be first must be your slave - just as the Son of Man did not come to be served, but to serve…. Matthew 20:26-28 NIV

Tony Akaki

11

Tony Akaki

21

Tony Akaki

Tony Akaki

29

35

Tony Akaki

41

45

Bibliography

Constitution of the Republic of Uganda, 1995

The Code of Conduct for Members of Parliament Rules of Procedure Parliament of Uganda

The Holy Bible

The Holy Koran

Leadership Code Act (Amendment) Act, 2017